Meet Shel Silverstein

S. Ward

The Rosen Publishing Group's
PowerKids Press™
New York

Published in 2001 by The Rosen Publishing Group, Inc.
29 East 21st Street, New York, NY 10010

First Edition

Book Design: Maria Melendez

Photo Credits: Cover, title page, p. 9 © AP/Wide World Photos; pp. 4, 7, 15 © The Everett Collection; p. 6 © CORBIS; pp. 8, 14 © Archive Photos; p. 10 by Thaddeus Harden; pp. 12, 19 by Myles Pinkney; p. 20 by Pablo Maldonado; p. 22 © Yann Arthus-Bertrand/CORBIS.

Grateful acknowledgment is made for permission to reprint previously published material on pp. 11, 16, and 21: *Where the Sidewalk Ends* copyright 1974 by Harper, used by permission of HarperCollins Publishers, written and illustrated by Shel Silverstein; *The Light in the Attic*, copyright 1981 by Harper, used by permission of HarperCollins Publishers, written and illustrated by Shel Silverstein; and *Falling Up: Poems and Drawings*, copyright 1996 by HarperCollins, used by permission of HarperCollins Publishers, written and illustrated by Shel Silverstein.

We extend a special thank-you to Waring Magnet Academy of Science and Technology for its participation in this project.

Ward, S. (Stasia), 1968–
    Meet Shel Silverstein / S. Ward.— 1st ed.
        p. cm.— (About the author)
    Includes index.
        Summary: A brief biography of the author of "The Giving Tree."
    ISBN 0-8239-5709-8 (alk. paper)
        1. Silverstein, Shel—Juvenile literature. 2. Authors, American—20th century—Biography—Juvenile literature. 3. Children's stories—Authorship—Juvenile literature. [1. Silverstein, Shel. 2. Authors, American.] I. Title. II. Series.

    PS3569.I47224 Z93 2001   00-022376
    818'.5409—dc21
    [B]

Contents

J-B
SILVERSTEIN
270- 2671

he Giving Tree

shel silverstein

In 1964, Shel Silverstein w... book called...

Shel was a well-known cartoonist.

the Giving Tr...

friendship betw...

the tree

man it...

old an...

story t...

a boo...

shel silverstein

iving Tree. The Giving Tree tells the s...

shel silverstein

The Giving Tree

In 1964, Shel Silverstein wrote a book called *The Giving Tree*. Shel was a well-known **cartoonist**. He was a good **musician**, too. Shel became known as a great **author** of books for children because of *The Giving Tree*.

The Giving Tree tells the story of the friendship between a tree and a boy. The boy plays under the branches of the tree and eats its apples. When the boy grows up to be a man, the tree gives him its branches to build a house. Then the tree gives the man its trunk to make a boat so he can travel. When the man grows old and tired, he returns to rest on the stump of the tree.

◀ *Shel Silverstein's simple story about the relationship between a tree and a human being touched the hearts of many readers.*

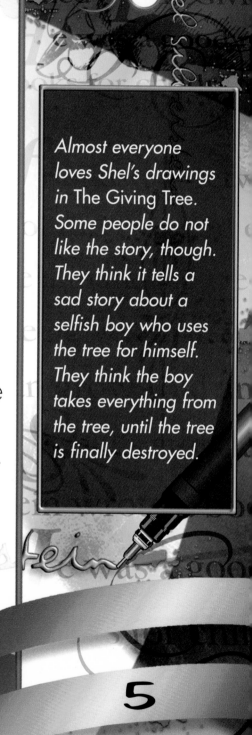

Almost everyone loves Shel's drawings in The Giving Tree. Some people do not like the story, though. They think it tells a sad story about a selfish boy who uses the tree for himself. They think the boy takes everything from the tree, until the tree is finally destroyed.

5

Baseball or Books?

Shel Silverstein was born on September 25, 1930, in Chicago, Illinois. As a child, he was good at drawing and writing. In 1975, Shel explained the way he began to make pictures and stories. This is what he said:

"When I was a kid—12, 14, around there—I would much rather have been a good baseball player or a hit with the girls. But I couldn't play ball. I couldn't dance. . . . So I started to draw and to write."

This is how Chicago looked when Shel was born.

Shel began to write and draw when he was a young boy. In 1979, Different Dances, a book of his drawings, was printed. ▶

Silverstein

Different Dances

he Giving Tree
In 1964, Shel Silverstein
iving Tree. The Giving Tree tells the
shel silverstein

Artist and Musician

In the 1950s, Shel served with the United States military in Korea and Japan. He drew cartoons for the military magazine *Pacific Stars and Stripes*. When his military service was over, Shel returned to his hometown of Chicago. He got another job as a magazine cartoonist. He also began taking an interest in music. Shel made friends with folk musicians in Chicago and New York City. He began to make up his own songs.

A soldier fights in the Korean War. In the 1950s, Shel served in the United States Army and fought in this war.

Children's Book Writer

Shel's publisher is HarperCollins.

Shel did not plan to write for children. He had a friend named Tomi Ungerer who was an **illustrator**. Tomi knew a children's book **editor** named Ursula Nordstrom. Tomi brought Shel to meet Ursula. This is how he said he first felt about going:

"Tomi Ungerer . . . practically dragged me, kicking and screaming, into Ursula Nordstrom's office. And she convinced me that Tomi was right; I could do children's books."

Shel thought Ursula was a great editor. She knew just how to help him with his writing. He started to write books for children.

Shel's funny poem "It's Dark in Here" and its illustration were printed in his 1974 book, ▶ *Where the Sidewalk Ends.*

IT'S DARK IN HERE

I am writing these poems
From inside a lion,
And it's rather dark in here.
So please excuse the handwriting
Which may not be too clear.
But this afternoon by the lion's cage
I'm afraid I got too near.
And I'm writing these lines
From inside a lion,
And it's rather dark in here.

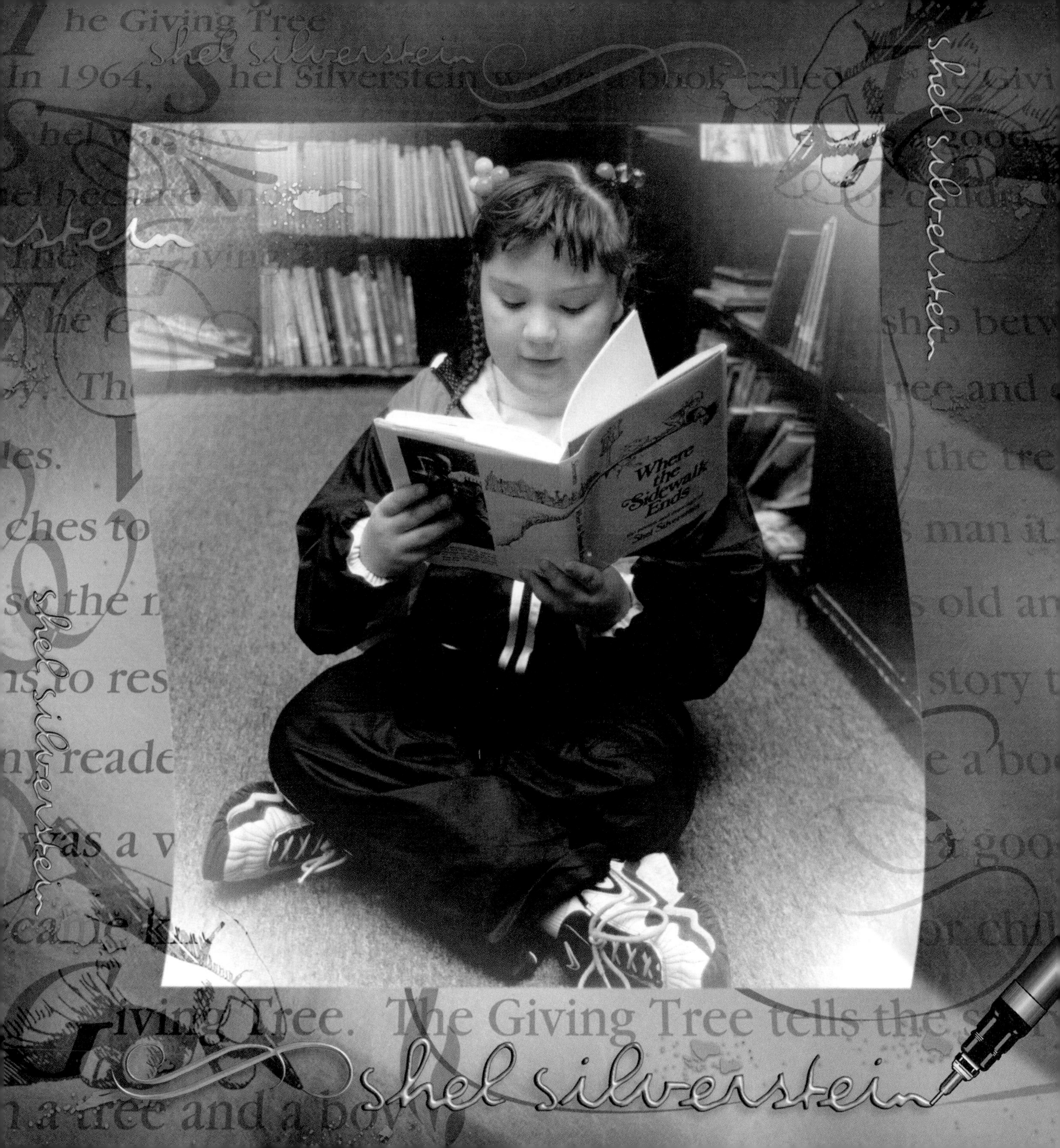
Where the Sidewalk Ends
shel silverstein

Writing for Everyone

In 1964, when Shel wrote and illustrated *The Giving Tree*, a book editor, William Cole, said that there was a big problem with the book. He said that the ideas in the story were too grown-up for children, but not grown-up enough for adults. Cole did not think anyone would buy the book.

Shel believed in his story. He did not worry whether children or adults would like it. One thing Shel said about *The Giving Tree* was:

"I would hope that people, no matter what age, would find something to identify with in my books. . . ."

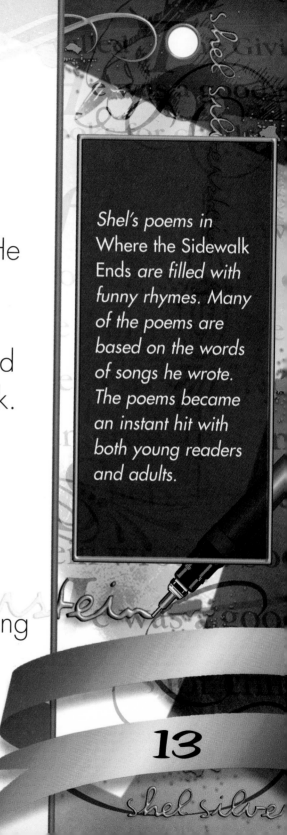

Shel's poems in *Where the Sidewalk Ends* are filled with funny rhymes. Many of the poems are based on the words of songs he wrote. The poems became an instant hit with both young readers and adults.

◀ *This child enjoys reading one of Shel's books. Some people thought Shel's books were too grown-up for children.*

Songwriter

Shel did not have a great singing voice, but he was very good at writing songs. Many famous singers liked his music. Johnny Cash, Loretta Lynn, Jerry Lee Lewis, and other well-known singers of the 1960s and 1970s sang Shel's songs on their records. Two of his most well known songs were "A Boy Named Sue" and "Hello Mudduh, Hello Fadduh."

Shel also wrote the music for four movies. In 1988, he wrote a song called "I'm Checkin' Out" for the movie *Postcards from the Edge*. He was **nominated** for an Academy Award in Music for this song.

Shel loved to play the guitar.

The actor Dustin Hoffman and Shel Silverstein are shown on the set of a 1971 movie. Shel often ▶ wrote music and songs for movies.

shel silverstein

MUSICAL CAREER

She wanted to play the piano,
But her hands couldn't reach the keys.
When her hands could finally reach the
keys,
Her feet couldn't reach the floor.
When her hands could finally reach the
keys,
And her feet could reach the floor,
She didn't want to play that ol'
piano anymore.

A Private Life

Shel Silverstein was a very private person. Many people loved Shel's work and wanted to know more about him. Shel did not like to talk about his work. In 1975, he finally agreed to talk to Jean F. Mercier. Jean wrote an **article** about Shel for *Publishers Weekly* magazine. One of the things Shel told Jean was:

"Lots of things I won't do. I won't go on television because who am I talking to? . . . Twenty million people I can't see? Uh-uh. And I won't give anymore interviews."

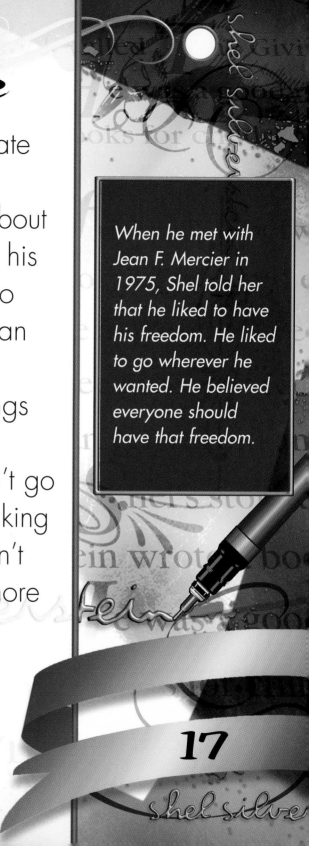

When he met with Jean F. Mercier in 1975, Shel told her that he liked to have his freedom. He liked to go wherever he wanted. He believed everyone should have that freedom.

◀ *Shel's special drawing style is shown in this illustration of a little girl at a piano. This drawing goes with his poem "Musical Career."*

17

The Missing Piece

Shel had a very different way of looking at things. In 1976, he wrote a book called *The Missing Piece*. The story was about a part of a circle searching for the piece that would make it a whole circle. In 1981, he wrote another book called *The Missing Piece Meets the Big O*. This book tells the story of what happened to the little piece that the circle could not find. Some people thought the two stories were sad. Others thought they were happy. Shel did not say whether he had meant the stories to be happy or sad. He wanted people to make up their own minds about his stories.

A teacher reads Falling Up *to a group of children at the library. Shel's poems include his views on* ▶ *animal rights and the different ways people act.*

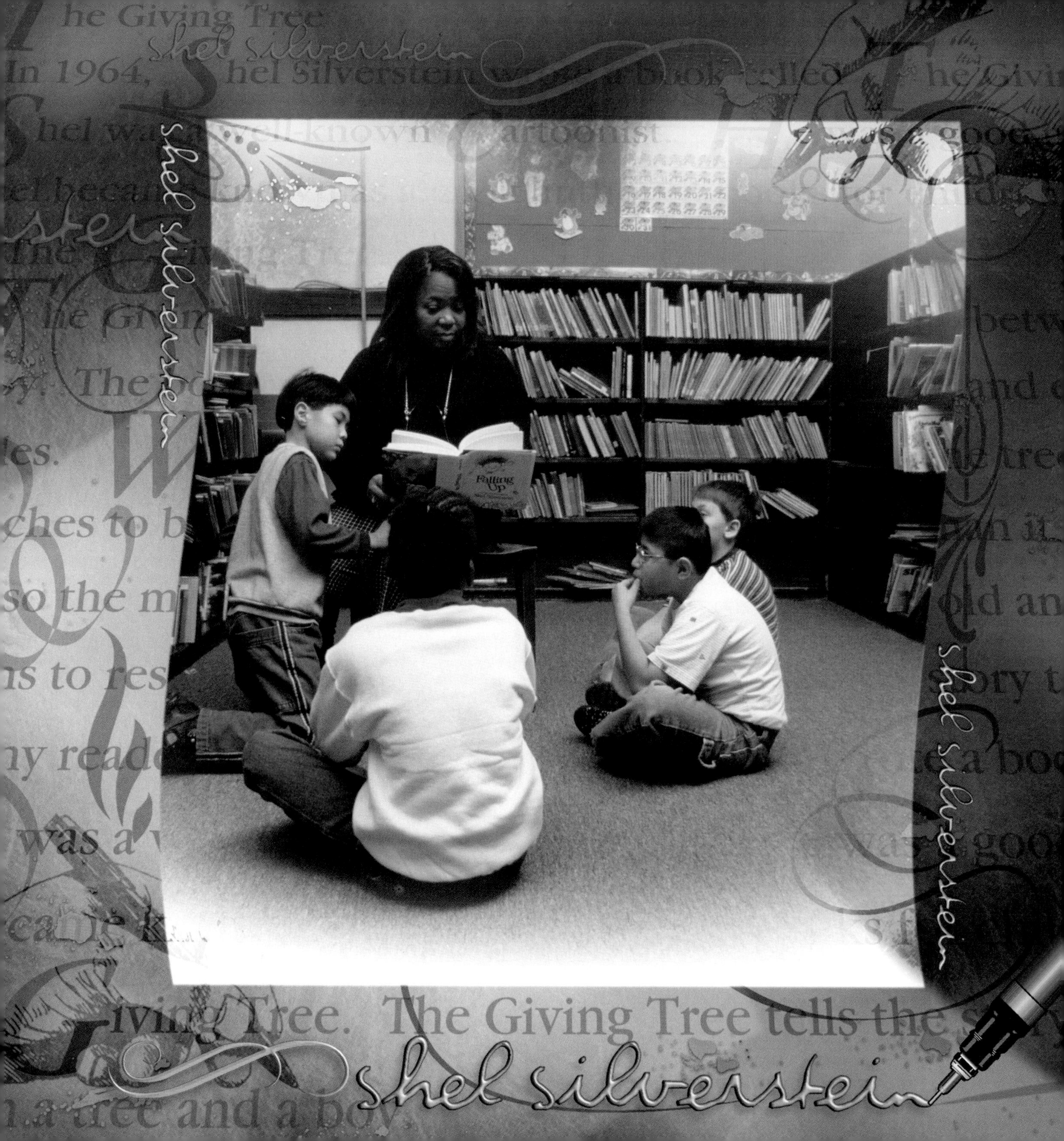

Falling Up

poems and drawings by
Shel Silverstein

A
Light
in the
Attic

poems and drawings by
Shel Silverstein

Where
the
Sidewalk
Ends

the poems and drawings of
Shel Silverstein

Poems

Some of Shel's most popular books are his **poetry** collections. He wrote three books of poetry. The poetry books are *Where the Sidewalk Ends* (1974), *A Light in the Attic* (1981), and *Falling Up* (1996). Shel illustrated these books with his own drawings. The poems in these books are funny. Many of the poems have fun rhymes. Shel's poems look at everyday things in new ways. Shel shows the silly side of growing up. Best of all, he shows where you can go if you use your **imagination**.

Shel's books of poetry and drawings became ◀ *popular with readers, young and old. Even most book reviewers liked them.*

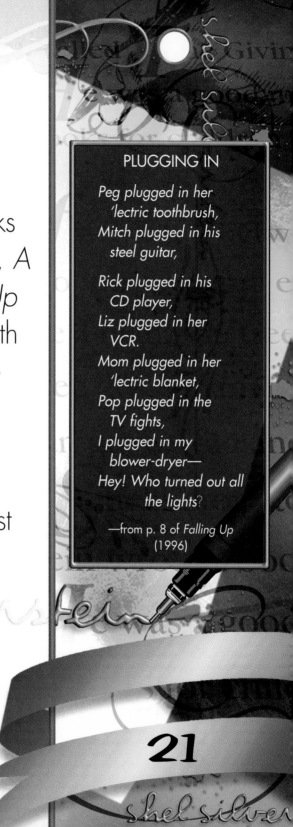

PLUGGING IN

*Peg plugged in her
'lectric toothbrush,
Mitch plugged in his
steel guitar,*

*Rick plugged in his
CD player,
Liz plugged in her
VCR.
Mom plugged in her
'lectric blanket,
Pop plugged in the
TV fights,
I plugged in my
blower-dryer—
Hey! Who turned out all
the lights?*

—from p. 8 of *Falling Up*
(1996)

21

A Full Life

Shel did lots of exciting things during his life. He wrote stories, songs, plays, and poems. He drew pictures and cartoons. Shel even wrote a movie. He lived his life in his own way and enjoyed it. Shel Silverstein died in Key West, Florida, on May 10, 1999.

Shel's life and books show that you do not have to choose just one thing to do. You can try lots of different things in your life. Shel once said:

"I want to go everywhere, look at and listen to everything. You can go crazy with some of the wonderful stuff there is in life."

This is the city of Key West, Florida.

Glossary

article (AR-tih-kul) A piece of writing for a newspaper or magazine.

author (AW-thor) A person who writes books, articles, or reports.

cartoonist (kahr-TOON-ist) A person who draws cartoons, which are drawings that make people or objects look funny.

editor (EH-dih-ter) The person in charge of correcting errors, checking facts, and deciding what will be printed in a newspaper, book, or magazine.

illustrator (ih-LUH-stray-tor) A person who draws or paints pictures that go with a story.

imagination (ih-ma-jih-NAY-shun) Being able to create things in your mind.

musician (myoo-ZIH-shun) A person who writes songs or plays music.

nominated (NAH-mih-nayt-ed) A person named as someone who should be given an award.

poetry (PO-ih-tree) Pieces of writing, or poems, that have rhyme or rhythm and tell a story or describe a feeling.

Index

Web Sites

To learn more about Shel Silverstein, check out this Web site:
http://195.114.233.19/Silverstein/SHELDONE.htm

shel silverstein